ARCHANGEL

David Marlatt

ARCHANGEL pg. 2

Smoothly, with Motion ♩ = 92

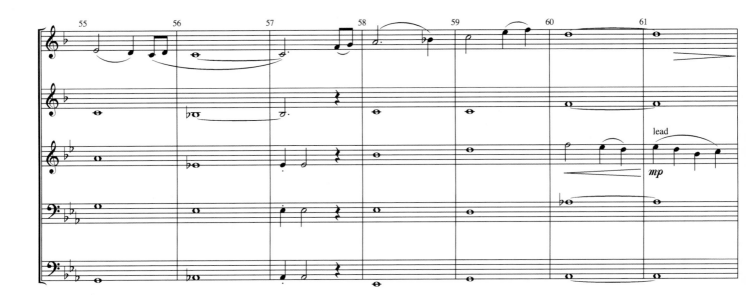

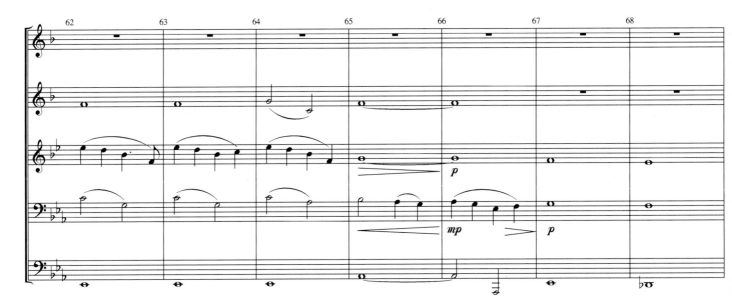

ARCHANGEL pg. 6

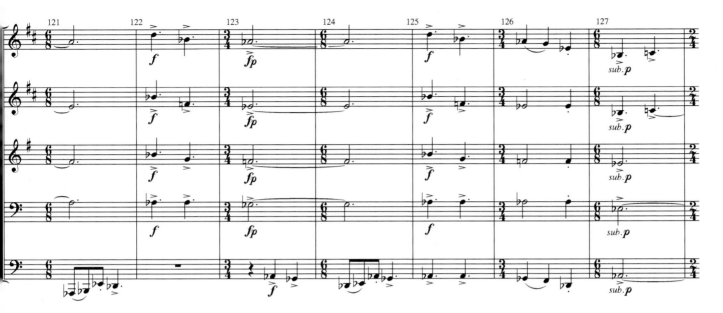

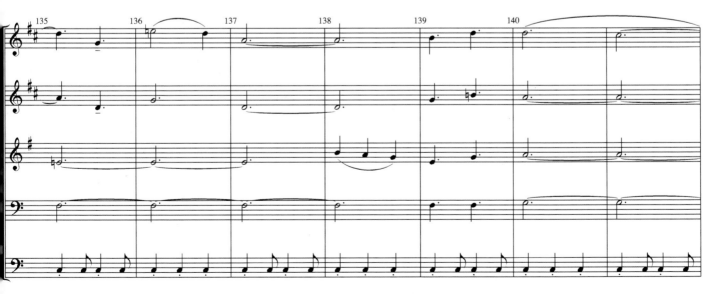

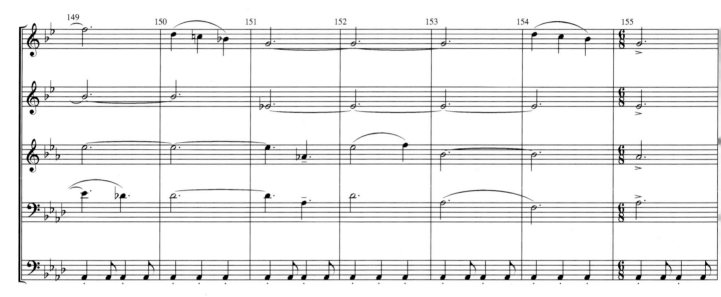

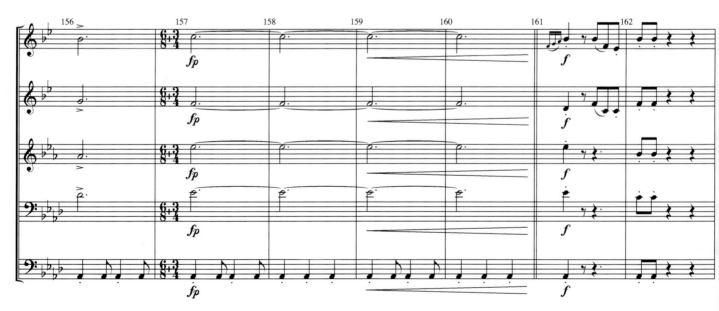

B♭ Trumpet 1

ARCHANGEL

David Marlatt

Bb Trumpet 2

ARCHANGEL

David Marlatt

ARCHANGEL pg. 2

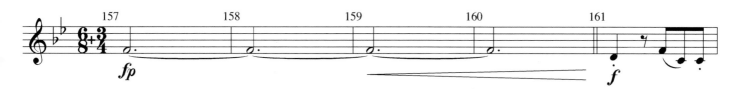

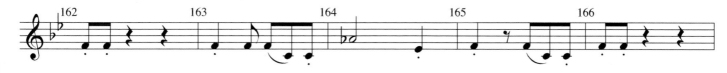

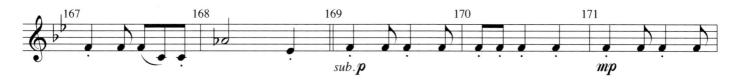

ARCHANGEL pg. 3

F Horn

ARCHANGEL

David Marlatt

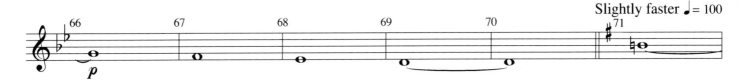

ARCHANGEL pg. 2

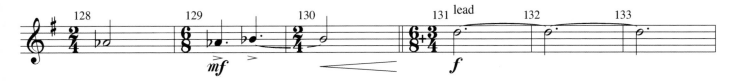

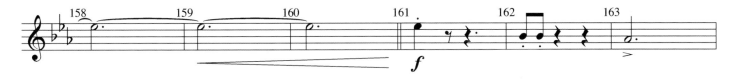

ARCHANGEL pg. 3

Trombone

ARCHANGEL

David Marlatt

ARCHANGEL pg. 2

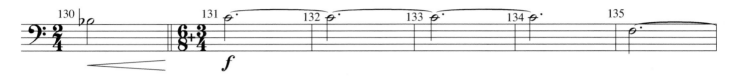

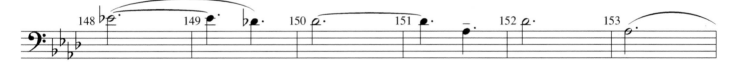

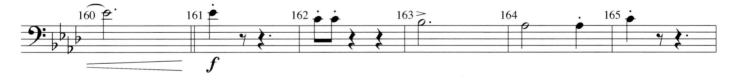

Tuba

ARCHANGEL

David Marlatt

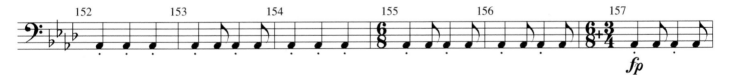

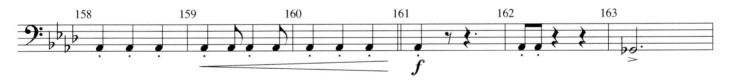

ARCHANGEL pg. 3